A YEAR AND A DAY

A YEAR

Poems by

Nashville 1963

and A DAY

Carlos Baker

VANDERBILT UNIVERSITY PRESS

Published in 1963
by Vanderbilt University Press
Nashville 5, Tennessee

To the editors of the following publications, in which certain of the poems in this collection first appeared, grateful acknowledgment is made: "First Light," Winter 1943, and "The Monkey House" (with the title "In the Cage"), Autumn 1943, *The Sewanee Review*. "Plane Coming," 22 January 1945, *The New Republic*. "The Hawk," "Calling In," "Dog Watch," "Two Worlds," "Night-Watch: Winter," "The Vigilantes" (with the title "All's Well"), Spring 1956, *The Virginia Quarterly Review*. "Design for a Tapestry," Spring 1958; "The Edge of the Tide," Spring 1959; "Sestina: The Garden" (with the title "Sestina at Forty-nine"), Spring 1960; "A Couplet of Herrick's," Summer 1962, *The Georgia Review*. "A Chinese Mural" (with the title "Words for a Time of Emptiness") and "Times Square at Twilight," Summer 1959, *Vox*. "May Day Rondeau," 1961, *All about the Symphony Orchestra* (Random House). "A Complaint of Mutability," Winter 1962, *The Massachusetts Review*.

Manufactured in the United States of America
Library of Congress catalogue card number 63–14645

*This book is for
Michael and Catherine*

AN OLD MAN'S WINTER NIGHT

(In Memoriam: Robert Frost)

That midnight hour he chose to go
Admonished weather-wiser men
To scan the iron sky for snow,
But we were none the wiser, then.

Like metaphor in tribute to
The poet we had lately lost
The morning sun he never knew
Spangled every tree with frost.

All day that day the blue sky burned,
A weather-breeder breeding woe;
At night the iron sky returned:
We watched our woods fill up with snow.

Out of all doors the fresh snow lies.
Indoors, his lap-board gathers dust.
He would not wish it otherwise.
He knew it must. He knew it must.

(January 1963)

CONTENTS

9

Part I

COMPLAINTS AND MEMORIALS

THE FOURTH OF JULY

(For Robert Frost)

What do you call that scarlet blur
That fills your field with smokeless flame,
Colored like courage? Tell me, sir,
What is its nature and its name?

The melting drifts of months ago
Could never now be lying here:
To call that second brightness snow
Ignores the season of the year.

Before the scythe, before the rake
Catch if you can that other hue:
Not fallen sky nor risen lake
Could make a color half so blue.

No. Devil's paintbrush, daisies, vetch
Will hardly do as names today
For what the romping children fetch
To make a patriot's bouquet.

A COMPLAINT OF MUTABILITY

(For William Carlos Williams)

O stop that running who are always gone when I come,
Or going, which is worse, for I see you before you
  vanish,
Hiatus wide as between Teutonic and Spanish.

O stop dissipating who are always becoming a cloud
In a cloudy memory, dissolving beneath the touch.
Stand still, stand quiet, or is that asking too much?

Too much, indeed. All those unimaginable sunsets
And dawns and stars and seasons, and all so fleeting,
Gone even when dates and hours were arranged for
  the meeting.

All those pears and those apples, bright like gold, like
  jade,
Pomegranates, avocados, all globed like satisfaction,
All gone and nothing left but an abstraction.

Those pies, those peaches, all those books, those games,
Those girls and those grouse in the woods, the ocean
  glistening,
Out of eyeshot and earshot for all our longing and
  listening.

Stop. But you will not stop. You have spun a long
   time,
Longer than Penelope, spinning, knitting, unravelling,
Or that husband who never seemed to tire of travel-
   ling.

THE MEN OF SUDBURY

(For and after H. D. Thoreau)

Greater, he called them, than Homer or Chaucer or
    Shakespeare,
Fuller of talk than a chestnut is of its meat,
Keeping their castles or chopping alone in the wood-
    lots;

Moving at morning through fields with their long
    ducking guns,
Wading with watertight boots in the fowl-meadow
    grass,
Hunting the teal and the ospreys, the black ducks and
    whistlers;

Men who were rude and sturdy, experienced and wise,
Clearing and burning and scratching the face of the
    earth,
Subsoiling, harrowing, plowing, again and again;

Only they never found time to set it all down;
They were never men who took to the way of writing:
Outdoors they were, outdoors every day of their
    lives.

Greater, he said, than Shakespeare or Chaucer or
  Homer.
But he was one who took to the way of writing.
The men of Sudbury move now in his pages.

SESTINA: THE GARDEN

(For W. H. Auden)

Here in this English bower bright with blossom
(White daisies, roseate white of pear and apple),
The year turns round once more, the mold is burst,
Fat dandelions brim the lawns with gold,
Green chaffinch builds, the redbreast plucks a worm,
Thrush cracks his garden snail against a stone,

And I, long-wintered now, long for that stone
(Philosopher's or alchemist's) fit to burst
The carapace and flood the world with gold—
Not flood, no. Yet before the final worm
Consumes the core that shapes the flesh of the apple,
I long to learn still other lore of blossom.

For what have we unless we have the blossom?
How otherwise achieve that golden apple
Which will not yield to challenge from the worm,
Being as durable as English stone—
Which nothing, not the beak of time, can burst,
Nor ever tarnish, being absolute gold?

I think of Keats and El Dorado's gold;
That urn, that other thrush, that perfect blossom
Frozen to music, and autumn plump with apple;
Of Wordsworth dreaming on his English stone

While round his head another Maytime burst
Whose flowers hid, but could not halt, the worm.

Like Coleridge, he was conscious of the worm
That lurks in darkness at the heart of blossom,
Or feeds on flesh of the fairest-seeming apple;
That—coiling blindly underneath the stone,
That—spoiling for whatever is not gold,
Waits the decay of all that time has burst.

The sun descends. Can fall, like springtide, burst
Or afternoon yet ripen into gold?
Is dust of pollen ready in the blossom
Even as it fades and falls to feed the worm?
Shall we, before we stretch beneath our stone,
Have years of light enough for the golden apple?

At seven times seven the apple has its worm,
Yet there is time, perhaps, for gold to burst,
Or stone, like flowers on English walls, to blossom.

(Oxford, May 1958)

COMPLAINT OF THE
ARTLESS SAILOR

(For Wallace Stevens)

How slovenly she slops along,
All awaddle, side to side,
Humming tin-pan-alley song,
Odorous of something fried,
Even something that has died:
So, ho, my green, my fluent mundo!

How lubberly she lumps along:
Broken shoelace loosely tied,
Shirt unbuttoned, skirt on wrong,
Yellow-brown hair sadly dyed
Like a white lie badly lied: *my mundo.*

How stubbornly she tubs along,
My love, my gross, my slippery world,
Drifting out of reach of song,
Purling coming half-unpurled,
Permanent come half-uncurled: *my mundo.*

How lovely-loose she leaps along
By all the blooming breezes hurled

Beyond my reef. What sailor's strong
Enough to keep, being whipped and whirled,
That Brobdingnagian belly furled
Of—O, *my green, my fluent mundo?*

HOLY WEEK: ITALIA

(For Donald Davidson)

··{ I }··

We knew it was Italy because of the people
Who carried the baskets and fagots and urns of water
Straight on their heads like pastoral coronets
Back to the tumbled casas up narrow alleys
Where bedding blossomed like flowers from upstairs
windows.

We knew it again because of the loud congregations
In every piazza of black-suited uncles and cousins,
Clots in the rain crowded under a single umbrella,
Palms spread, each finger expressive, gesticular,
pointed,
The umbrella-owner-and-holder impatiently tongue-
tied.

By the brown-pink-blue-green-pastel-stucco towns
Climbing irregular steps to the crown of the duomo,
Those crazy, brick-colored roof slates weighted with
stones,
The grass and the moss on the walls, lean cats on the
prowl,
And the red-sweatered dark signorinas strolling in
pairs
To catch and ignore the shouts of the cavalieri,

And the young mothers kissing the cheeks of bam-
binos loudly

With the sound a wine cork makes coming out of a
bottle,

And the storekeepers dropping their shutters from
one until three:

We knew it was Italy because of the people.

··{ 2 }··

And the signs said "Lavoro in corso"; they said "Ral-
lentare";

"Sempre Esso," they boasted again, "al vostro servi-
zio";

As for Roma, they said, it lies that way nineteen kilo-
metri,

Beyond it, Siena, Firenze, Bologna, Milano;

To the south, Napoli, old Paestum and newer Sa-
lerno,

And farther, Calabria's mountains where women
walk barefoot,

And hedges are cactus and stables are built out of oat-
straw,

And the oxen in dove-gray and burros in red leather
harness

All sprinkled with bells which will tinkle the same
Easter Sunday

As they do for the Sunday of Palms, for this breed
knew the honor

Years ago of transporting Our Lord to the gates of
the city.

In the Good Friday towns that were named for a hun-
dred saints,
Still wearing their bloody fleece, hanging up by the
heels,
The paschal lambs dripped small as earless rabbits;
And the old men, gravid with wine, let go in the
corners,
Rich with the richness and stench of two thousand
years;
While the moss-chinned gods spat water into the
fountains
The bedlam boys loud and proud at the wheels of
macchinas—
Rocco by name, or Pietro, or Salvatore—
Klaxoned their way round the mud-colored sheep in
the highways
And the mule-drawn carts with big wheels on their
way to the market;
While brown in their decent black the old wrinkled
signoras
Watched votive candles gutter in draughty chiesas
Where the Crucifix wore its coat of purple velvet
Until Buona Pasqua could lay its chocolate eggs
And the chick of new hope be hatched for one year
more.

Part II

A YEAR IN THE FIELD

Theme: Vigilance
Time: Then, now, later

THE HAWK

The brazen-footed hawk above the wood
Banks silently, and silently the sun
Tips beak and claw as with that creature's blood
Whose day was done before this day was done.

As he the ground, so we scan heaven for change—
Hawk's-eyed, yet groundlings chiefly—one with
    those
Who wait the stranger known as worse than strange:
A sudden air-borne shadow skimming close
To merge impossible fantasy with fact,
To rend surprise in two and hold the prize
Before reaction can defeat the act
Or premonition show monition wise.

Here, bloodied only by the sun, we stay
In waiting for what does not come, but may.

PLANE COMING

Now felt, beyond the yammer of the dogs
And raucous parliament of guinea hens,
Beyond the broken choiring of the frogs
And nickering colt beside the pasture fence;
Through all the air-softened clamor of the land—
Slammed door, spark trial and stutter, starting roar,
Dim parting cry, staccato reprimand,
Or laughter welling up from one word more—
Farther than these, yet knowable to the ear
Which gropes past nearness under the skin of night,
An operant probe, prepared for what is there
Ever before the sought-for comes to light:
That humming deep disquiet in the sky
That bloods all surface sound in thundering by.

CALLING IN

So the report runs. So the word is said—
(The singing wire takes the short song best):
"One plane, bimotor, low, heard overhead,
Out of the northeast, flying due southwest."

We do not say: "This is the kind of night
Wool makes a warmer blanket than the snow;
Three in the morning is no time to fight.
Suppose we call it quits, pack up, and go"—
Or "Looking up, with hands bent round our eyes,
We could not see the monster for the sleet,
Though we have taught our ears to recognize
That gross, explosive, guttural, double beat."
We give direction, type, and height instead:
"One plane, bimotor, heard low overhead."

THE WATCH CHAIN

Being only paunched and watch-chained citizens,
Seconds to Chronos, links new-forged for the task,
Hour-hands, not minute-men, in the defense,
Still ignorant, unschooled, and afraid to ask,
We try to do about as we were told:
To see, to say, to read, and to record
And—readier and steadier than bold—
To keep the Book according to the Word.

If ancient history like Lexington
Applies, the new Revere rides down a wire
To move indicative buttons, and is done
Without the need of stirring from his fire
As this long watch chain, linking sun to sun,
Lights one by one the lanterns in the spire.

DOG WATCH

The transient dog who came to try our love,
Preëmpt our private armchair like a throne,
To curl his muddy curls beside our stove
And lick our broken bread for lack of a bone,
Was one of those for whom the watch was kept.

What tramp, which of the brotherhood of monks
He represented where he laxly slept,
What savages, what children, or what drunks,
What tattered treasure in the terrible wind,
What snoring slumberer in another's bed,
What hopeless innocent, what heedless hind,
We never asked him, and he never said.

Yet for his bootless joy, his fruitless right,
We stared the stronger through the transient night.

TWO WORLDS

O lift of silver in the lofty air,
Translucency of wings there, high, way high,
Deluge-descent of drone-beats downing where
We stand way low—of earth as they of sky.

We know their drift who lack the downward look
To border sand beside the corduroy sea,
To wrinkled pastures ragged at the brook,
To movement merged to immobility.

Yet their monotonous eminence of place
Negates the lesser noise, the varied grain
Of what on earth we recognize as good:
We own the silence and enough of space
To seize, in happy consciousness of gain,
The flight of deer within the flickering wood.

NIGHT-WATCH: WINTER

Invisible above the frozen field,
Inaudible as ice in seams of stone,
In ruthless action inwardly revealed,
Once more the arrow wind barbs deep to bone.

The demon cold, dispassionately borne,
Accepts the tribute of our uttered breath,
Vanishing slow above the ruined corn
Like a premonitory sight of death.

And down among the stubble, swept of snow,
The scattered vertebrae of animals lie,
Unwatching eyes, reproving from below
The warden stars in the perpetual sky,
Both powerless, being past power, to do what we
Conceive the task of vigilance to be.

THE WATCH FACTORY

The worker seasons, laggard to begin,
Set Janus near the door to punch the clock
While, one and one, the others straggle in,
Nor deign the brief announcement of a knock.

O demos-months, we know your palpable tricks,
Have known your faces, bent a patient ear
To all your squabbles, lent a hand to fix
What March left broken in his mad career,
Smiled May, talked June, and slapped July away,
Supped from the pail of August; seven to ten,
Watched Romans carry apples, wood, and hay,
And, one to twelve, pass through our door again
While we, the tabulators, keeping score
Remain in mute possession of the floor.

THE VIGILANTES

Now ring the bell, call in the passing plane
Which carries home the signatures of peace.
Now close this door, domesticate again,
And revel in the racket of release.

Now scrape before your mirrors, build your roads,
And watch your children laughing in the sun,
Accept this here, this now, obey your codes,
And do unto your neighbor what is done.

Yet know: beards grow, the jungle will encroach,
The unwatched child may stare beneath the wheel,
The near and dear recede, the far approach,
The neighbor-nation fabricate in steel.

Another hand may ring the watchman's bell,
An alien tongue proclaim that all is well.

Part III

A DAY IN THE CITY

There now is your insular city of the Manhattoes, belted round by wharves as Indian isles by coral reefs . . . Circumambulate the city on a dreamy Sabbath afternoon. . . .

Herman Melville
Moby-Dick

A MIDNIGHT VIEW OF THE CITY FROM FIVE THOUSAND FEET

Far east, past Ambrose, nicors swim
West of the dim
Adjacent light;
Far west, the monster ranges hold
The privative cold,
The primitive night.
Down here men sleep
In dark as deep
As ever the sounding serpents know;
Down here men lie
As silently
As on the western peaks the snow.

··{ 1 }··

FIRST LIGHT

Not now full-blooming glut of day,
But updawn of ubiquitous light
In which one universal gray
Inaudibly obscures the night,
While negatives to ear and eye
Develop their antitheses:
From silence, birdsongs multiply
And, black on lessening dark, the trees.

··{ 2 }··

THE OLD BURYING GROUND
NEAR THE SCHOOLYARD

Among these leaf-emplastered mounds
And shrubs where green besieges gray,
The quickening shout of children sounds
Unnecessarily gay
Because the opposite estate
Of mouldering and of budding leaf
Sooner than joy can demonstrate
The uselessness of grief.

··{3}··

THE OLD MAN ON THE BENCH IN THE PARK

This old red dog rocketing down the green
And slanting turf pretends the youth he begs,
But after, somnolent by the fire screen,
Will rouse himself for nothing on four legs.

This eighty-year-old, being spare, being dry,
Pursues retreating bodies, not too far,
With pursing lips and distance-squinted eye
As an astronomer pursues a star,
Begging a youthfulness he'll not pretend
In coin of what he once knew how to spend.

··{4}··

THE LOVERS ON THE GREENSWARD

How many angles they and I,
In limited liberty to choose,
As vertices can occupy:
Right, isoscles, obtuse,
Equal, linear, scalene;
In various quick mutations we
Make manifest upon the scene
Those figures from geometry.
All, all, the measure of all,
Draws to the mathematical.

When zero overspreads the brain
To end the speech of eye and lip,
How mutely shall we then maintain
Triangular relationship.
All, all, the measure of all
Sinks to the mathematical.

··{5}··

RUMINATION IN A PUBLIC PHONE BOOTH

How delicate innocence grows thick,
And how the turn of sweet is sour.
Minim stick and magnum sick
Is penny-minute's pounding hour,
And snuffer to the flaming wick
As flowering frost to flower.

··{ I }··

THE MONKEY HOUSE

Darwin's dæmon, Barnum's pride,
The razor-fanged misanthropist
Scurries up and down to hide
The orange in his yahoo fist.

Archetype of ancient greed
By a present greed beset,
In whose gestures one can read
What he would as soon forget,

Clio's child will stop to chew
All his craft cannot conceal,
Cram full cheeks and then outspew
Fragments of the pulp and peel.

Gaily as he perpetrates
Evolution's epigrams,
Mocking those he emulates
And by his emulation damns,

This scion of a present past
Argues for the world's great age
And triply underscores the vast
Monkeyhood of the master sage.

··{ 2 }··

THE SNAKE PIT

In these raptorial kingdoms
Whose strategy is strife,
What noon has borne by two is torn
To lead another's life.

The alimentary kingdom
Encloses like a ring
The right of might until the night
Evolves another king.

··{ I }··

ENCOUNTER IN THE
READING ROOM

Poet (musing):

> In all of entomology
> What is more somber
> Than gadfly that pretends to be
> A heavy bomber?

Critic (musing):

> We crowned him King Unmidas
> To signify the gross
> Deliberate way he operates
> In turning all to dross.

Poet (playing with notions):

> I saw, because my eyes were bent
> Upon the hard gray pavement,
> That gout of spilled ink, black and wet,
> Where someone's bottle had overset—
> And caught there, pushed there by the breeze,
> A rime of blossom from the trees.

How light it made my heart to think
That poems are blossoms caught in ink.

Critic (playing with rhymes):

Gross . . .
Dross . . .

·{2}··

A COUPLET OF HERRICK'S

"Die, ere long, I'm sure I shall,"
Wrote Herrick, brooding on his fame,
"After leaves, the tree must fall."

Yet trees turn logs, logs kindle flame,
And, Herrick, in the spreading dark,
Note this commemorative spark.

··{3}··

GEORGE WITHER

Wither, punning on his name:
"I grow and wither both together."
Time's a plant no pun can tame:
Wither could not tame it, either.

··{4}··

MAY DAY RONDEAU

(For François Villon)

Sing welcome to the merry month of May;
Farewell December sleet and April rain:
We have the sun to soothe us warm again.

Now all the flowers say what flowers say
In blessed springtime after winter's bane:
Sing welcome to the merry month of May;
Farewell December sleet and April rain.

We are so certain spring has come to stay,
Ignoring all the laws of human pain
How witlessly we warble our refrain:
Sing welcome to the merry month of May;
Farewell December sleet and April rain:
We have the sun to soothe us warm again.

·{5}·

A FAREWELL TO LOVE

(After Chaucer)

From Love I leaped in hope of growing fat
Within whose clutches I had grown so lean:
To me (at last) Love is not worth a bean.

If Love should argue, saying this or that,
The only thing I'll say is what I mean:
"I leaped from Love in hope of growing fat
Within whose clutches I had grown so lean."

Since he's withdrawn from me the welcome mat,
I'll just erase his name, too, for I mean
To make this break both permanent and clean.
Now I've left Love in hope of growing fat
Within whose clutches I had grown so lean,
I know for certain Love's not worth a bean.

·{ 1 }·

DESIGN FOR A TAPESTRY

Under these flowering apple trees she lies
All sweet and easeful, somnolent and still,
As unfallen Eve, ascending Eden's hill,
Found velvet turf, felt sleep attempt her eyes,
And wondering whether she might sleep her fill,
Lolled, stretched, and yawned, her hands behind
    her head
Unscarred, unscared, on that sequestered bed,
And presently felt sleep lift through her will
Until she slept—and dreaming thought she saw
A shape of evil lowering in the skies,
Contracted all her muscles as to flee
The acid vomit and the smoking maw,
And screaming waked—but laughed to recognize
The friendly serpent on the hillside tree.

·{2}··

A CHINESE MURAL

The Master said: "The Fang bird does not come;
The river sends forth no map. All's over with me."

In the time of Wan they gambolled in the hall;
In the time of Wan they sang on the slopes of the
    mountains.
They only sing when the sage ascends his throne;
They only sing when the right is going to triumph.

When the dragon-headed beast with the stallion's
    body
Rose out of the river with diagrams on his back,
Fu-hsi was able to read and understand.
Fu-hsi interpreted. Fu-hsi grew wise.

The Master said: "The Fang bird will not come;
The river contains no map. All's over with me."

··{3}··

ON A LANDSCAPE OF SESTOS

Behind him spreads the horizoned shore
Of satisfactions earned and granted:
That cleanswept house with open door,
The graceful trees that he has planted.

Salt and sick, this young Leander
Swims for Sestos' greener fields
Looking for sweeter oil and blander
Than the olive ever yields.

Sick and salt, in love, in hate,
Clambering up this island rim,
He knows the fires in the strait
Have burnt the fire out of him,

Yet seeks beneath the cloven mountain
That temple of another race
Where by the leaf-chocked inner fountain
Hero waits with she-goat's face.

··{ 1 }··

THE VIEW FROM A SKYSCRAPER

Offshore, along the always there
Still blue and blue of sea and sky,
As meant to seize and hold astare
An ever-seaward-ranging eye,
The silent southbound ships go by;

While here, unmoved, the ever land
Lies anchored vast a third between
A plane of sea that ends in sand
And one of sky that starts in green
To bend aloft, incarnadine,
Across the intermediate air

And flowing down from growing height
To set those moving ships aglare
Until last golden flakes of light
Burn out upon the nil of night.

·{2}·

THE OLD MAN TAKES HIS SUPPER IN THE FRONT WINDOW OF THE AUTOMAT

To murder ignominious months and days,
To certify that the dead hour has died,
To bury, burn, obliterate the phrase,
The deed, the lust, the ignorance, the pride;
Not to invite propinquity with prayer,
Cement disclaimed relationships in stone,
Or, tangled in a garland of bright hair,
To white the sepulchre of whiter bone—
So has he wished.
                    Still the unsummoned faces
Of old and greener ignobilities
Enforce their presence, elbow to their places,
Nor wonder that their host is ill at ease.

He knows his portion ashes and gall. They start
A eucharistic banquet on his heart.

··{3}··

TIMES SQUARE AT TWILIGHT

Now light upon the looms of stone
Weaves soundlessly in gold and red,
Before our history is done,
A pall for all the decent dead,
Tomorrow's disinherited—
Till night across the glooming stone
Reveals in current golden O's
The history of what was done
That man may measure all he knows
Before, like yesterday, he goes.

··{4}··

INCIDENT UNDER THE ELEVATED

After the monster met him and he fell,
Gray in the face as a fog is gray in the face,
For a moment the ragbag under the legs of the El
Diverted the monster-stream from the midst of
    that place.

Under the beams in the basement of guttering day
The light burned out before the lights came on;
Repairmen who came to carry the rags away
Saw nothing to linger for and were presently gone.

Once more, above, the train of realities
Moved in, made pause, and moved out, while below
    once more,
The oblong murderous monsters with meaningless
    eyes,
Having no reason to pause, streamed on as before.

·{5}··
THE END OF THE SHOW

While for a while those highest windows hold
Luciferous the glamor of his gildings,
See sun now sliding down his golden wire
High from his perch on cornices of buildings
As
    acrobats
           glide
                downwards
                      bearing
                          fire,
And grounded watch the lower lights burn bold
Now that the higher braver light is gone.

In some such wise the city night comes on.

HAMLET TO THE SKULL OF YORICK

Like one dissatisfied to go,
Having incompletely said his say,
Of everything I think I know
This is the knowledge bound to stay:

Not that the wielded sword is good,
Nor yet the wound, nor even dry
Deep agony, nor hardihood
Of active ear or hand or eye;

But that such bone immures a field
Where two or three have entered in
To fight, and all but one must yield,
And, without triumph, one must win,

And I must always say, "Begin."

·{ 1 }·

THE DUMP

Junk, jetsam, hell to skelter come
Rots in this corner pared from Dis,
And rats the size of tomcats roam
Where never a jot of herbage is;

Where wags this rigor-mortised cur
Draped in the virgin's bloody skirt
And nailed him to (the final slur)
This post above the crawling dirt;

Where Dante, drawing near, would know—
His sandals rank with human mire—
How needful here, as still below,
The golden cautery of fire.

··{2}··

THE EDGE OF THE TIDE

All this he knew before:
What palpable shade
Pools under tide-racked straws
By moon; these lightly-made,
So-soon-erased, bird-caused
Small tracks; gull strut and soar;
But most, nomadic stone,
Abandoned spiral house
Beside the hundredcolored heave of sea,
Which now in him would rouse
All irrevocably
Outgone, outgrown.

COLOPHON

THE TEXT *of this book is set in twelve-point Caslon Old Face, three points leaded. The title page and display matter are set in various sizes of Caslon Old Style. These are type faces belonging to the Old Style group cut early in the eighteenth century by the great English typefounder William Caslon. Modelled on Dutch types of the seventeenth century, Caslon's designs far surpass their originals in interest, delicacy, and variety. Essentially English, and therefore rather less elegant than the characters of the greatest French designers, they have a beauty of proportion and a serviceable quality perhaps unequalled by any other type face.*

The trademark was designed for Vanderbilt University Press by Theresa Sherrer Davidson. It is a form of the triskelion, a device which, besides appearing in the arms of both Sicily and the Isle of Man, has been employed by many cultures, one form of it by the Indians of Tennessee. The Fugitives, the group of poets who flourished at Vanderbilt in the early 1920s, adopted it informally as their emblem. The symbol was originally three legs joined together, and to the Fugitives it was evidently seen as three legs running. It also bears a relation to certain sun symbols and may have signified the light the Fugitives were seeking, for they saw themselves as fleeing towards *as well as* away from *something. In some representations the triskelion is seen as three V's joined together. Theresa Davidson is the wife of the poet Donald Davidson, several of whose books she has illustrated.*

The book is printed on Warren's Olde Style laid finish paper, manufactured by the S. D. Warren Company of Boston, and bound in Columbia Mills Riverside Linen. Typography and binding design are by Paul Randall Mize.